This Creatures of the World Series
Book belongs to:

____

In the Rainforest, You'll Find Me

is a great book series to begin your journey of learning about the different types of animals in the world.

Thank you for your support.

This book is dedicated to:

Haley,

Our biggest dreams for you are that your never afraid to dream big! Open your mind to all this life can offer and love this life wide open. With love larger than life we love you.

-Mom & Dad

Scarlett,

My beautiful granddaughter who we love since the day we found out we would be grandparents. You will always be our blessing and will love you to the moon and beyond.

-Love, Belinda

This book is dedicated to:

Reno,
   You are more than I ever expected and better than I ever imagined.
                                                             Reno & Debra
Camila,
      Never forget that this world is beautiful, especially now that
                              you're in it!
                                                       -Love, Tia Daniela
Cameron,
        Be curious, adventurous, kind, a light in the dark, be you.
                                                       -Love always, Mom

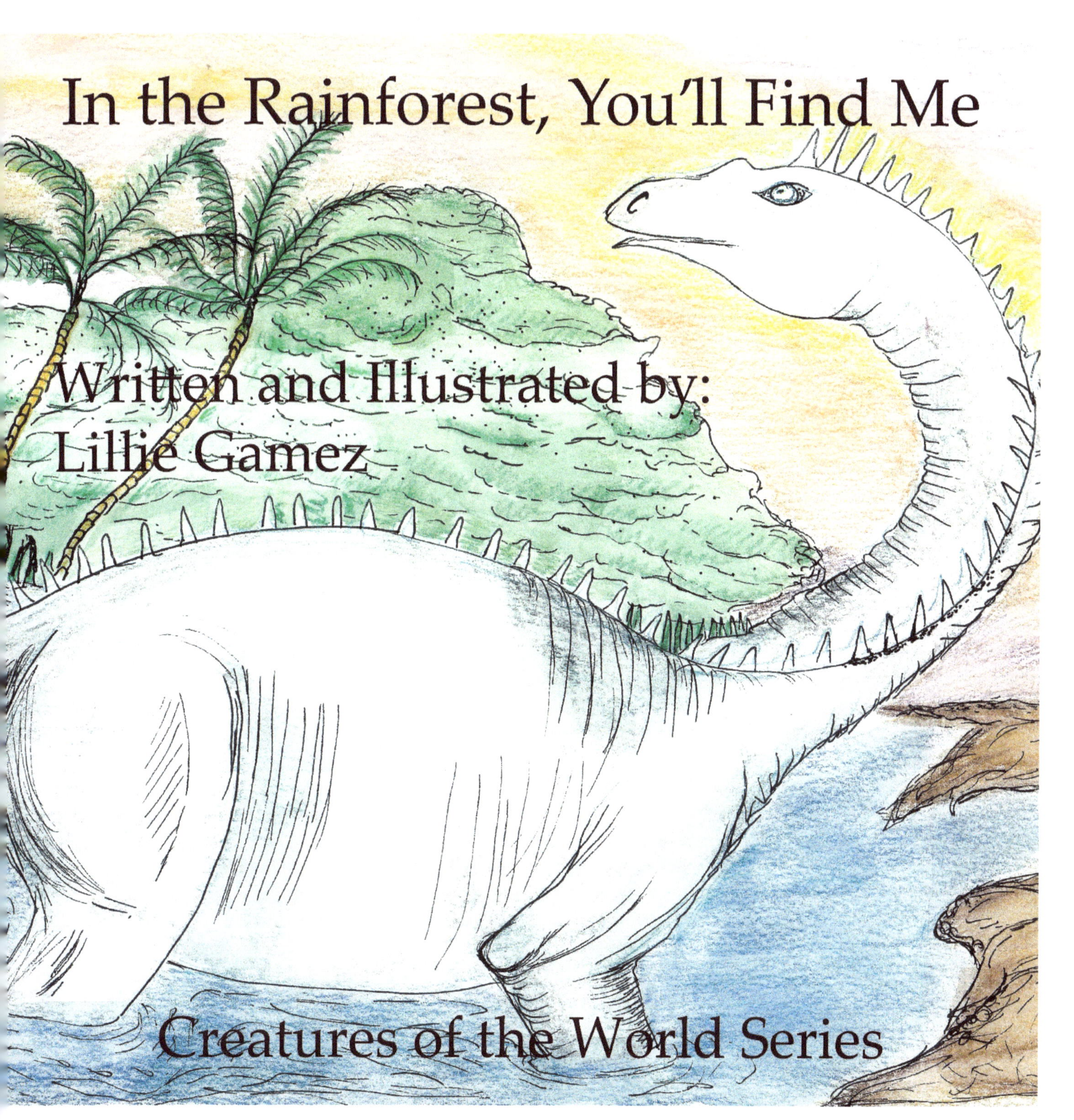
In the Rainforest, You'll Find Me
Written and Illustrated by:
Lillie Gamez
Creatures of the World Series

In the Rainforest, you'll find
me hiding in the leaves. I am
a master of disguise. I use
my bright colors to scare my
predators away from me.
I am the Red-Eyed Tree Frog.
Can you find me?

In the Rainforest, you'll find
me. Living with my family in
the hollows of a tree in the
rainforest canopy. I have
small wings so I can't fly to
far. I like to hop and use my
claws to hold on tight with
all my might to find food in
the trees. I am a Toucan,
Can you find me?

In the Rainforest,
you'll find me moving
oh so slow up in the trees.
I can sleep up to fifteen
hours in a day.
I love to eat leaves,
twigs, and bugs.
I am a Sloth.
Can you find me?

In the Rainforest, you'll find me in the water, so happy. I am the largest and most powerful snake in the world. I grow longer and longer all my life. I swallow my food whole and can birth as many as twenty to forty babies.
I am an Anaconda.
Can you find me?

In the Rainforest, you'll find me. On the ground, I'll be roaming around in search of delicious bugs that I will make mine. Look at my snout its long and can fit into small places to find the tiniest ants to eat.
I am a Giant Anteater.
Can you find me?

In the Rainforest, you'll find
me. Living high up
in the trees. My limbs, hook
like fingers, and long tail keep
me hanging and climbing way
up high.
I love to eat seeds,
fruits, and flowers.
I am a Spider Monkey.
Can you find me?

In the Rainforest, You'll Find Me. Hiding in trees, waiting to pounce on any prey that comes my way. I have lovely spots that are shaped like black roses all around me. I am a fierce Jaguar. Can you find me?

In the Rainforest,
you'll find me swimming
in the Amazon river.
I am electric when I hunt
or am feeling hunted.
I shock my prey so I can eat.
I am a Knife Fish but they
call me the Electric Eel. Can
you find me?

In the Rainforest, you'll find me
during the Jurassic period. Weighing
as much as a large truck all while
eating only bushes and trees. I use
my heavy tail to balance me. I am a
dip-lod-ic-uss. Can you find me?

Draw your favorite Rainforest

Creature in the space above.

To all the artists who will make their mark.
Never give up your dreams and always work for them.

The Author and Illustrator of this wonderful Creatures of the World Series is Lillie Gamez, a retired Art Teacher hoping to inspire families everywhere to love animals and create their own works to share with the world. Although born and raised in Del Rio, Texas, Gamez received a Bachelor's degree of Fine Arts in Photography from Texas State University. She is currently homeschooling her two young children and using everyday life as inspiration to create her next series. You can also find her teaching art at different local community centers. For more information about her services check out her website at

www.OnlineMamaG.com

and sign up for the next event near you.

Don't forget to share your drawing online #OnlineMamaG and post to

@OnlineMamaG